I0419939

DYING TO EAT, EATING TO DIE

Learning to survive compulsive overeating, depression, anxiety and obsessive-compulsive disorder

Marianne Catherine Joyason

ISBN: 1540506827
ISBN 13: 9781540506825
Library of Congress Control Number: 2016919594
CreateSpace Independent Publishing Platform
North Charleston, South Carolina

TABLE OF CONTENTS

PREFACE

I realized the truth about my life when I was about thirty years old. I was eating uncontrollably, but I did not know why. What I *did* know was that if I did not stop, then I would die. After some therapy, I was diagnosed with obsessive-compulsive disorder (OCD), depression, anxiety, and compulsive overeating. Although I was highly successful in the world, I had this internal struggle. What follows is my story: how I got there; what happened as a result; my treatment, struggles, successes, and failures; and how I eventually started living my life again.

CHAPTER 1

THE EARLY YEARS

For as long as I can remember, I was a heavy person—obese. When I look at childhood pictures of me, even as a baby and a toddler, I was heavy. I remember my pediatrician telling my mom at every visit I needed to lose weight.

Hating my body image and myself started for me at a very young age. There are certain parts of my childhood that are very vivid for me. These parts (I realized after many therapy sessions) were the most influential in shaping my disorders and issues.

My dad was the joy in my life when I was growing up. Everything I did was to please him and make him proud. I would help my dad with projects. I would help him at his work. The two of us did a lot of things together. I was more of a son to him than my brother was. I knew he loved me even though he never told me he did—at least I thought he did.

Dad owned and operated an Italian restaurant and pizzeria. Mom would take us kids over to see Dad at the restaurant almost every day, and he would make us pizza. These are some of my fondest memories of my father. Many nights, I would stay up until midnight and wait for my dad to come home from work. We would share a pizza and watch late-night television. For the longest time,

I was a late-night person, and pizza was one of my biggest comfort/binge foods.

My dad worked very hard and long hours. I remember walking home after my eighth-grade graduation because he had gotten a call that the restaurant was very busy, and they needed him. Dad missed most of the ceremonies, concerts, plays, and awards presentations I participated in because he was always working. Mom would say that Dad worked in order to buy me nice things, so I felt guilty that I was angry toward him for missing these events.

My mom was a homemaker, but I was never really that close to her growing up. She was college educated but stopped working after having my sister, her first child. I remember my dad and my mom fighting a lot. My mom never seemed happy. Dad was not into buying gifts or cards for holidays, and Mom used to complain to me about it. For a couple of Christmases, my dad gave my cousin money to buy my mom gifts, but she never liked any of them. She sent them all back because Dad did not pick them out. She was never pleased. Looking back now, I realize she was depressed.

My mom called me one day about six years ago and asked if I would stop at the house because she had a few things to give me. She asked me if I wanted the designer purse I had bought her four Christmases ago. She had never used it; it still had the tags on it and the receipt inside. She also asked if I wanted the bracelet that I had bought her ten years ago as another Christmas gift. It too had the tag on it. As a result, today, I do not like Christmas or buying presents. I fear I will buy the wrong gift, and the recipient will hate it.

Mom's discipline consisted of her saying, "Wait until your father comes home." As soon as Dad would walk through the door, my mom would start complaining. Dad would look so tired. At times when he was really annoyed with us, he would beat us with his belt. We would cry, and I felt ashamed. I felt I was a bad person to deserve those beatings. For years, I would tense up and step back when anyone tried to hug me.

When I was a kid, my mother always made a big deal about cutting the sizes out of my clothes, which were never modern. She also did not like me to carry around bags from the larger-size clothing stores. She would tell me not to tell anyone where I bought my clothes. Everything was a secret. This made me feel ashamed and different. Still, to this day, I do not like shopping for the aforementioned reasons.

I remember two mother/daughter conversations I had with my mom. One was when I was in the eighth grade, when I was the only girl who did not make the cheerleading squad. I believed it was because I was fat. Mom came into my bedroom where I was crying and tried to comfort me. I do not remember what she said, but it was the only time I felt she cared. I felt close to her at that moment. The other time was when she talked with my sister and me regarding sex. I remember all three of us were uncomfortable. I asked my mom where babies come from. She told me when two people love each other, they have a baby. That was our first and only sex talk.

My mom was always very critical of us children. She would make negative comments about our clothes, hair, or just about anything she could think of. She was very controlling.

I can remember taking family vacations as a kid; we visited many places. Dad and Mom never took a vacation for just the two of them. They always included my sister, my brother, and me. Mom would tell Dad not to tell anyone we were going on vacation because it was nobody else's business. I recall leaving home to begin our vacation at twelve or one in the morning after Dad had worked a full day. My parents would fight over not making reservations. Mom would say they were not needed. She would say you should not plan for tomorrow because you do not know what today might bring. Dad would say reservations were needed. Mom would win. After driving for a while, we would look for a hotel, and sure enough, there would be no vacancies. She and Dad would argue, and that would set the tone for the rest of the vacation.

My mom always asked us kids if we were hungry when we were out in the car. We always said yes, even if we weren't. My dad would stop at fast-food places, but Dad and Mom would never get anything to eat. Dad would not want to spend the money, and Mom would not eat because Dad did not. Then when we got home, Mom would complain she was hungry. Fast food, especially hamburgers, was another type of food I would binge.

My sister, brother, and I were taught many lessons and grew up with values. We were told to always respect our parents and elders. We were taught to obey everything our parents said because they were always right. We were told never to question them. We learned to never throw food away and to finish everything on our plates, because it was a sin to waste food. We had to finish everything whether we were hungry or not. If we did not eat everything, then Mom would be hurt that we did not like her meal.

I was sick a lot as a child, suffering from colds, sore throats, and earaches. I was also very clumsy growing up, so I had a lot of accidents. I have since learned that these are characteristics of a person with obsessive-compulsive disorder (OCD).

In my house, everyone always seemed to be mad at one another. There was no communication. I became the joker. I felt that my role as a child was to keep the peace and to make sure everyone was happy.

Dad used to complain to my mom about our house being a mess. My mother never put anything away or threw anything out. If company came over for a visit, then my mom would get mad. She hated company. We were embarrassed to bring friends over because our house was in such disarray. I used to clean our house as a surprise to my parents when they would go out. I used to spend hours cleaning the downstairs. When they came back home, I would ask them what they thought of my work. I was looking for a thank-you or praise for doing a good job. Instead, they would ask why I had not cleaned behind the couch or some other section I had forgotten. They were never pleased. Nothing I did was ever good enough. The house would be a mess again the next day. As a result, I became, at least for some time, very compulsive about the cleanliness of my own house.

My siblings also had their share of problems as well. They were overweight and had strained relationships with our parents. My mom was at a healthy weight when she married my dad, but after she had her first child, she became obese. My dad has been heavy all his life. He had a heart attack at the age of fifty-eight due to stress and high cholesterol. My mom's parents were overweight, all my mom's siblings are obese, and my father's family is also heavy.

Exercise was considered a waste of time in my house. Working was stressed. Neither of my parents had a life of their own. My dad did not believe in watching much television or talking on the phone. He never relaxed, and my parents never had fun. We were told we were lazy if we were just sitting around. The motivation to do well has made me very successful in life, but it has also made me stressed. Now I know there has to be a balance. I had to learn that scheduling time to relax was just as important as scheduling time to work.

I was raised Catholic and attended church every Sunday until the time I reached the age of thirty. I went to a Catholic grade school and high school. I was taught that if I would trust in God, then he would protect me. I also was taught that if I were bad, then God would punish me.

I became used to not receiving compliments. When I was in school, I would get 100 percent on my test, and my parents would say they expected grades like that from me. Once, when I did not get a 100 percent on a test, my dad asked what was the matter with me; he said 98 percent was unacceptable. I was embarrassed. The irony was that my brother and sister did not get good grades, but that did not seem to matter to my parents.

I never had a boyfriend in school. I never went on a date. I never went to the prom. Nevertheless, I was popular because I was funny. In eighth grade, my classmates voted me the "class clown."

Throughout elementary and high school, my best friend was Judy. She was very skinny. We did everything together. We were called "spaghetti and meatball," skinny and fat. Mom used to say not to worry about the name-calling. I pretended it did not bother me, but it did. I laughed off everything that hurt me.

I had a lot of male and female friends in high school. I was involved in many clubs and nonathletic activities. I would try to get out of gym class, though, because I was embarrassed to change in front of the other students, and I also didn't want to show how easily I could become winded. Because of my asthma, my mom used to write me excuses to get out of gym class.

I remember having junk food drawers in our house. Everyone constantly went to the drawers and ate. I recall going to them ten, fifteen times a day. Most of the time, it was just to look through the drawers and check what was in them. I would memorize the order of the items. Then I started to sneak and eat the food. I would leave only one or two items in a package so I would not be accused of eating the entire bag. I would do this the day my mom went food shopping.

Another early memory of compulsive behavior I can recall was when I was fifteen. My family and I went on vacation. My aunt had bought me a pair of gold earrings, and somehow, I lost them on the plane on the way home. My mom yelled at me and told me I was irresponsible. She called the airline for a month looking for the earrings. For the next ten years, she brought up the fact that I had lost them! My mom had a lot of beautiful jewelry, but she did not wear any of it. She was afraid of losing it.

After that trip, I began to count the jewelry that I wore. I would do this ten to twenty times a day to make sure I did not lose any pieces.

Food was such a focal point in my childhood. I have only one memory of my grandmother, and it revolves around food. That memory is set in her bakery, where my aunts, cousins, mom, and grandmother sat around a long, rectangular table. We were making homemade ravioli.

In our house, food was used in good times and in bad. We actually had a relationship between good and food and sad and food. If we were good, then we got to visit dad, and he would make us a pizza. If we were sad, then we ate junk to stuff the feelings.

I do not blame my parents for my disease. I do wish they had done some things differently, but I am sure they did the best they could at the time. I feel, as you get older, you cannot blame others; you are responsible for your own life. My background did, however, help to shape my disease.

CHAPTER 2

THE COLLEGE YEARS

I graduated from high school with high honors and many accolades. The award I valued most was for outstanding character, which was voted on by my peers and teachers. I was so proud of myself.

I wanted and was expected to go to college. I knew I was the child who had to make my parents proud. I had to shine. I had to be the successful one.

I will never forget the first day of college. I was so scared being alone in my dorm room. I found out many years later that my mom had cried all the way home after my family dropped me off. Yet she never showed any kind of emotion toward me that day or any other day, until much later in my life. Never an "I love you" or an "I am proud of you" from either one of them.

My college years were tough. I would stay up all night studying for tests. I never felt I knew the material well enough. I actually memorized chapters of books because I had reviewed the material so much. I would check essays and reports over and over again to make sure they were perfect. I thought this was normal behavior. I never knew this was OCD.

I went to a few parties while in college, but I always felt out of place. I never felt I looked nice. Heavy people's clothes were not the style. Guys would talk to my friends—but never to me. I ended up being everyone's friend. I was the mother figure. I took care of my friends when they had a hangover or were sick. I was the person they could most rely on. I felt responsible for everyone's happiness. I tutored people and became the president of my dormitory. I was fun to be around. I was the good girl.

On the inside, however, I was hurting. I started hiding in my room more and more as the years went by. My weight grew higher and higher.

In January of my sophomore year, I transferred colleges because I was so depressed, my grades were suffering, and my OCD was terrible. On top of that, my weight was rising. I used to skip lunch and dinner, and then I would order out from my dorm room when no one was around. I always ordered pizza. I would eat the entire pizza and throw away the box in the hallway. I got really good at sneak eating and hiding the wrappers. My friends thought I never ate. I would eat "good" in front of them when I did eat, or I would deprive myself.

I graduated college with honors. I heard only a "We knew you could do it" from my parents. I was fortunate to land a job immediately. I was so happy! I finally loved my life, and I loved my career. I decided to do something about my weight, which was at an all-time high. For the first time in my life, I began dieting and started to lose weight. I was thrilled.

My home life was another story, though. I hated living with my parents after being on my own in college. I tried to clean up after my mother and brother. Then my father would come home from work and say I was lazy and should help around the house more. He never saw what I did—only what I did *not* do. He was always yelling at me. My weight started to climb back up, and I got scared.

CHAPTER 3

SEEKING HELP

I joined a fitness center and went from not exercising at all to doing two aerobics classes and working out with weights daily. (I did not learn until later that OCD manifested itself into many areas of my life.) I lost pounds and inches, and I was feeling good. But I would stay at the gym real late so I would not have to face my parents at home.

A few months later, the weight came creeping back. I panicked. What really scared me was that I was starting to hate my job. This, for me, was my rock-bottom moment. The one thing in my life I had been really happy with was starting to make me unhappy. I could feel myself sinking into a pit, but I did not think I could afford to seek help because I was not making a lot of money.

Because I knew my insurance would cover it, I went to a nutritionist. I went to her looking for a quick cure; what I got, instead, was a miracle. I told her I wanted to go on a liquid diet, but she told me the center no longer offered the program because many people were gaining the weight back—plus more—when stopping the meal-replacement shakes. She also said people were having some medical problems as a result.

I was devastated. The nutritionist advised me to begin a food diary, but I knew that would not work. I told her exactly what and how much food I should be eating. She asked me why—if I knew what to do—was I not doing it. That was exactly what I wanted to know.

She said to give it a week, so I did. I still ate what I wanted within that week, but I did write everything down. When I went back to her, I had gained weight. She took me into her office and asked if I would consider speaking to a therapist. I told her I really wanted to but could not afford one. She told me about a therapy agency where, for the first visit, I was to bring my pay stub, and they would determine my rate based on my salary. I was so relieved—but also scared. I thought I was a crazy person, having to go see a therapist. I believed only "crazy," uneducated people saw therapists.

With determination to finally get healthy, I made an appointment with a psychologist. It was in another county because, of course, no one could know my business, and I was ashamed, but I made the appointment. My therapist determined that I was suffering from chronic depression and was a compulsive overeater. We had many great sessions during which I revealed a lot about my home life. When she first asked me about my feelings, I did not know how to respond. I had never expressed or identified feelings before, so I really couldn't articulate them, because I didn't know what they were. She thought it would be best if I tried to remove myself from my home environment. I agreed but could not afford to move out.

She gave me a lot of literature to read regarding my disease. Between my love of reading and the OCD, I finished most of the books within one or two days. One book particularly caught my attention. It described a woman going through problems that were similar to mine. She talked about seeking help at an eating disorder clinic, so I asked my therapist about this idea. She and I both felt it would benefit me, and she started looking into it for me.

Meanwhile, I never told anyone I was seeing a therapist. I was embarrassed and felt alone. I felt like somehow I was less of a person. But one day, my mom was going through my dresser drawer in my bedroom while I was at work. She found my appointment card for my next therapy session. Of course, she never came right out and asked me directly about it. Instead, she said things such as "I hope you're not doing anything to risk your job...You know if you go to talk to someone, they will tell people, and you will be fired... Any problems you have should stay in this house." Needless to say, I received no support. I knew better than to listen to her, because it just depressed me more.

My therapist found me an eating disorder clinic in Florida. I was scared but excited about going. I told my mom—only in case there was an emergency. As I expected, she was mad. She said it was a mental illness clinic, and they were going to plant all kinds of ideas into my head. She told me she was going to lie about where I was going to my dad, because his heart could not take the truth. That made me feel very guilty.

I will never forget those feelings I experienced as I was leaving for the trip. My mom dropped me off at the airport; we barely said two words to each other. I was so nervous. I boarded the plane, sat down, and barely fit into the seat. I had never felt so alone. I was twenty-five years old, but I cried from that moment until well into the night after I arrived at the clinic. I felt like a loser.

I remember entering the center and looking around in the lobby. *There is an awful lot of security*, I thought to myself. When they took me up onto the eating disorder floor, the reality finally set in. I *was* in a mental hospital. I thought I must be crazy. They had lied! Certainly, I had never heard of compulsive overeating, and I did not know anyone else who had had it either.

The first thing the nurse did was to search my suitcase. She made me give her any sharp objects that I had packed. I was numb. I asked her where all the other patients were. She informed me I was the only one there at the time.

During the first couple of days at the clinic, I had intensive one-on-one therapy. It really helped. After that, three other people joined me: another compulsive overeater, an anorexic, and a bulimic. Together, we all worked very hard at getting well. I learned a lot about my disease and myself. I was taught I could control it. I also learned that people with bulimia and anorexia suffer from the same types of problems as a compulsive overeater. They, however, choose to deal with their food in a different way than people who overeat. But we all had distorted images of our bodies.

A typical day at the center for me was waking up at 7:00 a.m., showering, and taking medications. Then we would go down to the cafeteria for breakfast. We would have group counseling and individual counseling. After lunch, we would have recreational therapy. At night, we went to Overeaters Anonymous meetings.

The worst time for me at the clinic was when there was family therapy on the weekends. The other patients were from Florida, and their families came to visit them. They were very supportive. I thought of my family, and it made me sad.

In the end, it turned out that the hospital was exactly what I needed to get started on the path to being healthy. I entered the hospital at my highest weight: 265 pounds.

After five weeks and the loss of a couple of pounds, I was discharged and on my way back home. I felt scared but strong.

CHAPTER 4

ON MY OWN

The first thing I did when I got home from the clinic was to look for an apartment. My dad would not talk to me, and my mom was convinced that "those people" had put the idea in my head at "that place." But I was not discouraged. I found an inexpensive apartment. I took my bedroom set and got a free family-room set from friends.

A few months later, I turned twenty-six and was down to an all-time low in my weight—160 pounds. I was a size 14/16 and buying clothes in regular stores. I was poor, but I had never been happier or healthier. I swore I would never put the weight back on. I would not relapse. I got rid of all my large-size clothes (even though my mother told me to keep them for when I gained all the weight back). I was happy and confident. I even asked my first gentleman out on a date. I was feeling good. I was eating healthy, cooking for myself, exercising, and going to Overeaters Anonymous meetings twice a week.

Nine months later, I began my relapse. I had to deal with an ethical issue at work with an influential person. Because of this, I had to seek an attorney's advice. He charged me $100 per hour, which I could not afford. I had to take a part-time job at night, causing me to be exhausted. I started eating fast food again and stopped exercising. Food was the only thing that supported me. It made me forget. It blocked out my feelings.

After hitting rock bottom again, I sought help. I went to see a different therapist, who immediately suggested I see a psychiatrist for medication for my depression. I agreed and was diagnosed with chronic depression, anxiety, and OCD. I tried a few different medications until I found the combination that worked. They would seem to help for a while, but then the old feelings would start to come back. I also hated the side effect of sweating. I felt defeated and stopped going to both professionals. Once again, I was looking for a quick cure.

My depression mostly was due to the fact that I was alone, which I blamed on my weight. At thirty years old, I had never had a boyfriend. I had gone on five dates in my entire life. I had never been to the movies, gone for a romantic walk, or been out to dinner with a man. I felt like a freak, and I blamed it all on my being overweight. I had a lot of male friends—I was a great friend—and I heard these friends talk about other girls. I knew what they wanted, and it was not what I had. The only males I was close to were gay men and married men. I did not consider them a threat, because I knew they only wanted friendship from me. They were safe.

Family events, holidays, and birthdays started to become hell for me. I hated celebrating anything. It only reminded me that I was alone.

I isolated myself from my family and friends and wanted to die. I was committing suicide by food—I was feeding myself to death.

After about a year, I decided to go back for help. I found a different therapist, a nutritionist, and a psychiatrist. That was when I decided to write this book. I was thirty-some years old and weighed over 370 pounds. I wore a size 34, a 5X.

CHAPTER 5

FINDING ANSWERS

W hat I learned in therapy was that my behavior, including my eating disorder and depression, centered on my OCD. To get back some control of my life, I went on antidepressants, OCD medications, and sleeping medications (which I needed because my mind would not turn off when I went to bed). I also reflected on my past and noticed how OCD had manifested itself into my life in so many ways.

I was a perfectionist, and I had to be the best in everything. I finished my master's degree in two years. I completed eighty-six credits beyond my bachelor's degree in four years. I had never realized this was all part of being compulsive.

I was an anxious person. I made lists daily, going through lists and ideas in my head at least ten times a day. I overextended myself with responsibilities. I did not work well with others, because I liked to get things completed quickly and efficiently. I never wanted to rely on someone else. When I moved into my new apartment, I had everything unpacked and in its place in two days.

I tried to buy happiness. When I was making a low salary, I told myself that when I got a better paying job, I would be happy. Then there would be nothing for me to worry about. But when I *did* make more money, there was still a lot for me to worry about. I moved into a great new apartment, telling myself I would be happy when I had all nice furnishings. And I *was* happy—until everything settled down, and I realized nothing had changed. I was still fat and alone.

I was compulsive in my cleaning. Everything had to be in its place; all my pictures and decorations had to be symmetrical. Even in work, everything had to be in order, or I could not concentrate. Every time I would get out of my car, I would shake my car mats to get rid of the dirt. I would even shake all my mats if no one else were in the car.

I developed severe sleeping problems. I would sleep about two hours a night. As soon as I closed my eyes, my mind would race on all I had to do. I could not turn the obsessive thinking off. I could not sleep even with the sleeping pills, so they kept changing them.

I developed temporomandibular joint (TMJ) syndrome due to stress. I would grind my teeth at night, which necessitated my wearing a mouth guard.

Besides the two lists I had made, I also carried a calendar around with me. On days when I felt things were out of control, my lists would have twenty different things to do on them for one day. I would write items such as "get up," "take shower," and "get dressed" on the lists. After I completed something, I checked it off my list. I would cross the item out once, double-check it, and cross it out again. Then I would resort to check marks, sometimes checking an item off ten times.

I started being late for work because I had to go through the entire house multiple times to make sure everything was in order. I opened closets and drawers. I checked faucets. I even made sure multiple times that the car doors were locked.

Then there was my eating disorder. I would go food shopping once a week and steal food to eat while I shopped. I was a thief. When I got home, I would eat all the food I had just bought. I could not stand anything being in my refrigerator. I wanted to keep it clean and neat. I would open a bag or box of just about anything and eat the entire contents. This was true with healthy and unhealthy foods. I could not stand anything being left open and not finished.

I was a fast-food/mini-mart binge eater. I was a compulsive overeater. My hell would begin when I entered my car at the end of the workday. That is when my mind would switch to the mode of thinking that I was alone and probably always would be. I was going home to an empty house. I would make two or three food stops along the way home and eat in my car.

After I binged, I would feel sick and numb. The mind-racing would stop; the anxiety would be curbed. I would swear I would not do it again…but I always did. I obsessed about food. I got through the day by thinking of what I was going to eat for supper.

I tried all the diet trends. I bought pills through magazine advertisements that claimed to take weight off without exercise or diet. I went to a doctor who put me on prescription diet drugs. I lost five pounds the first week and gained seven the next. I inquired about over-the-counter liquid diets. I went on a fat-free yogurt and fat-free muffin diet. I lost lots of weight and gained it all back. I knew the weight did not come on overnight, but I wanted it gone overnight.

I was embarrassed to eat junk food in front of other people, and I would even hide the junk food in my shopping cart. However, most of my friends were overweight, so I loved to go out to eat with them. As soon as one brave soul said he or she was ordering something "bad," we all would. My one girlfriend loved to go out for an ice cream, but she would make us drive around so that she could finish the cone in the car. That way, the neighbors would not see her eating it, and no one would see the wrapper in her garbage.

The answer to my problem was to get the depression under control and *then* work on the anxiety and OCD. I had to let go of the weight issue, which for me was very hard. I also knew I had to work closely with my therapist on my issues. This time, I could not quit.

CHAPTER 6

SEARCHING FOR INNER PEACE

I wrote this book as a form of therapy. It started out as a journal and a way for me to put my emotions on paper and to examine them. It helped me to put my life in order and to see all the experiences I have gone through. It helped me to see how strong of a person I have become.

One huge step I made toward my recovery was to tell a friend about my problems. She was very supportive and nonjudgmental. It felt so good after thirty years to finally talk openly. I felt so much lighter!

I remember attending a wedding for my twenty-three-year-old cousin. I cried. I did not want to go. I had obsessed about the day since the invitation had arrived for the bridal shower. I could not help but wish it were me getting married. I had no one to escort me to the wedding. I was so depressed.

On some days, I would become very tired and agitated. I had thoughts of driving my car into traffic and ending my life. That was how overwhelmed I would become.

On days when someone or something made me angry, I would eat and eat and eat. I ate a dozen doughnuts, an entire pizza, a half-gallon of ice cream, or whatever I could get my hands on. It was my way of punishing that person or thing that had made me mad, even though I was only punishing myself.

Vacations were not fun for me. I hated getting my picture taken, because I did not want to see what I looked like. I had a mental image of myself, and when I saw pictures of me, I could not grasp how heavy I had become.

I remember one vacation in particular when I could not fit into the seat on the airplane. I had to use an extender in order for the belt to fit around my waist. I was embarrassed. Then, whenever we would use a taxi, I sat in the front since I took up the most room.

On the flight home, I was taken out of the emergency exit row because the stewardess stated that passengers who must wear an extender could not sit in the emergency exit row, as they were not capable of handling an emergency. Instead of getting angry like I should have, I was embarrassed and humiliated.

People do not realize how hard heavy people have it or the humiliation they feel daily. Being a heavy person has not been easy. Airplane seats, bus seats, bathrooms on buses, and waiting-room chairs with arms are all nightmares. Booths, car seat belts, and theater seats all made me nervous. It is a horrible feeling to have to go somewhere and worry if you are going to fit. I remember taking a trip to New York on a chartered bus and praying the entire time I would not get sick or have to go to the bathroom.

Discrimination was also a major issue. Most people look down on heavy people. I remember an incident when I went to a neurologist about my lower back problems. He told me the reason my back hurt was because I was fat. He told me to eat salads all day—that it was easy and not a big deal to lose weight. I wrote the medical board about him.

When you are heavy and you get sick, people think it is because of your weight and because you are not taking care of yourself. Willpower has absolutely, positively nothing to do with weight loss. Food is a drug. People think that is a joke, but it is true. I think excessive drinking is crazy. I drink every now and then, but I do not know how people become alcoholics or why they cannot stop drinking. But alcohol is their drug of choice. Food addiction is so visual because you wear the addiction on the outside. Drug and alcohol addictions are just easier to hide.

One day, my back went out while I was getting out of the bathtub. I fell on the bathroom floor naked. I crawled on my stomach to get to my phone. I had to call the paramedics to help me. When they came, they could not get me downstairs because my apartment had a windy staircase, and they would have had to lift me over their heads. I will never forget when the paramedics called for backup over the walkie-talkie. They had to call the firefighters in to help them. I can still hear them saying "We need backup. The patient is very large." It took two ambulance crews and a fire truck to get me down.

CHAPTER 7

RELAPSE AGAIN

Today is the first day of the rest of my life. At least that was what we were told in group therapy. I checked myself, under the guidance of my therapist, into a mental health hospital. I was having irrational thoughts and contemplating suicide. Probably the most important thing I learned there was that I was not alone. There were other people from all walks of life who had similar problems.

When I mentioned my preoccupation with my weight in group therapy, the others seemed shocked, as if I was being ridiculous. I felt relieved. I knew then that I focused too much on my weight. It was incomprehensible to me that other people did not care about my weight.

At the clinic, once again, I was at my rock bottom. I could not believe I had let myself get that bad. The worst part was telling my immediate family. I was scared, but they were supportive, although Dad was naturally quiet. The first night they came to visit, I kept asking them if they loved me. They said of course—but they never told me. I never heard those words.

The days there seemed very long and endless. They woke you up at 7:00 a.m., breakfast was at 8:15 a.m., and that was followed by distributing medicines and getting your vitals checked. Then there would be a community meeting followed by a morning session. Lunch would be served at 12:15 p.m. followed by group therapy at 1:30 p.m. Then, for those who could go off the floor, there was recreational therapy. I was not allowed off the floor since I had just arrived.

When I saw the dietitian, she informed me that my cholesterol was 320, which was very high. She put me on a low-cholesterol, low-calorie, and low-fat diet. It was easy to follow a diet in the hospital, because there was someone to cook for you. I weighed well over 375 pounds. I was too heavy for the scale to get my actual weight.

I remember one particular evening in group therapy. The topic was on love and relationships, a very difficult issue for me. I cried during that entire session.

The next day, my psychiatrist decided to increase my medications. I told her that I had signed myself out. This meant I could leave in seventy-two hours. I was worried about losing my job; I had told everyone I was ill and staying with my sister. My therapist was not happy with my decision.

I got released from the hospital the day before my birthday. I hated turning thirty-one and being by myself.

I saw my psychiatrist a week later. She changed my medications again because the depression was not easing up. I started working on being content with where I was in my life—just for today. I rejoined the gym and started working out three times a week.

A couple of months later, I learned to relax and realized that relaxing did not make me a lazy person. I changed my eating habits. I recognized when I was full. I still would not keep food in my house, but I was getting better. I hired a maid to clean my house so I would not obsess. I was feeling better, eating less, and was off the sleep and anxiety medications.

But when I got stressed out, I would retreat back to my OCD behaviors. I remember one weekend I spring-cleaned my house until 4:00 a.m. I would not stop until I was finished.

CHAPTER 8

GETTING TO KNOW MY DISEASE

Let me try to describe what a typical day was like for me when my OCD was at its worst. My alarm would go off at 6:15 a.m. At 6:30 a.m., a colleague of mine would call to check if I was awake. At 7:00 a.m., I would finally get out of bed. I always felt tired. I would rush around to get ready because I would be running late. I would sweat profusely, a side effect from the medications. Before I left my house, I would go through every room and check in each drawer and each closet to see what was in them. I would walk through with my list, making sure I had everything checked. I would then spend about ten minutes making my bed. It had to be perfect. I would leave my house at 8:00 a.m., checking over and over again to see if the curling iron was off and if the front door was locked. I would also check the faucets and the stove by turning them on and off before I left. By the time I arrived at work, I would be covered in sweat. Many times, I was late. I would go into my office and try to calm down. The first thing I would do was read the newspaper. I would read it over and over again to be sure I did not miss anything. I would go through my briefcase by taking everything out and check off each item on my list as I put it back in. I then ruminated on five lists in my head. I would picture my parents' house and would go through it room by room to see if I had forgotten anything when I moved out, which at that point had been more than four years earlier. Next, I would go through every room in my old apartment. Then, I would go through every room in my new apartment. Finally, I would go through my former office and then my current office to be sure that I had not forgotten anything anywhere. I also kept a pile of papers in my desk, which I would go through eight or nine times a day.

While doing my work, I would check my papers and then re-check them to make sure I had not made any mistakes. I would not leave work unless my desk was cleaned off and everything was in order. As I was leaving, I would check my mailbox. I would take my mail home, because I could not stand anything being left in my mailbox. On my way home, I would stop at many convenience stores and donut shops along the way to get food. I would eat in the car. In my mind, eating in the car did not count as real eating. I had no idea how much food I was consuming. I was numb.

As I got out of my car, I would check the front, the back, and the trunk to make sure that everything was in order. I did not want to lose anything, miss anything, or leave the car dirty. Once I was in my house, I would empty my briefcase and go through it all again. I would then recheck my house, opening every drawer and cabinet—including looking at the shelves in the refrigerator and freezer. I did the checking in a specific order every time. If at any time while doing my mental lists I was interrupted, such as to answer a phone call, then I would have to start all over again from the beginning.

After all the checking, I would do more office work. I would rewrite my list of things to do for the next few weeks, because I hated how sloppy the list looked when I crossed out items on it. I would try to fall asleep early because I was so tired, but my mind would race. I could not shut it off and would usually end up falling asleep around 3:30 a.m.

It is amazing how, when I got stressed or anxious, the OCD behaviors returned full force. I tried using behavior modification. My therapist told me that by checking, I was reinforcing the behavior and that checking did not really calm the anxiety. But when the feelings came over me, all I wanted to do was check the lists. I did become calm, but it only lasted a short while. I became sick and tired of being sick and tired. I decided to do a lot of research on OCD.

The reason I checked things was to avoid potential disasters. If I did not check the curling iron, then the house might catch on fire. If I did not check the lock on the door, then a burglar might break in. I repeated mental lists as a way of ensuring safety. I also checked to prevent emotional disasters. I did not want to be looked down upon by others. I did not want to be criticized for forgetting to do something or for doing something incorrectly. I was afraid to make mistakes. When you have OCD, discomfort arises when things are not perfect, which was why I used to hate it when anyone touched my belongings.

I liked to save old magazines and books, just in case I might need them someday. (This is called hoarding.) If I threw something away, then I would worry that I had made a mistake and might need it someday. Then I would go through my garbage to double-check that I had not thrown away anything important.

Other characteristics I possessed were the inability to tolerate uncertainty and imperfection. I was uncertain about what the future held for me, and this made me anxious. I also suffered from low self-esteem. I felt I was never quite good enough.

I felt an awesome responsibility to make everyone happy and to take care of my family and friends. I never once thought about my happiness or taking care of myself.

I hated going out to eat. I had to look through the menu completely, even if I knew what I wanted. If someone interrupted me, then I had to start over from the first item. I wanted to make sure I had made the best possible food choice.

Many days, I thought I was crazy—that I was losing my mind. I thought I was alone, and I was embarrassed and ashamed. I thought taking medication was a sign of weakness, but when I tried to cut down on the medications, my depression and OCD symptoms would return.

I knew which thoughts were irrational and did not make sense, yet I was unable to ignore those thoughts. For example, I would worry about my brother being in a car accident. Then when he was in one, somehow I felt if I had worried more, then the accident would not have happened.

I experienced a lot of self-doubt, especially regarding my job. Late at night, I would think that maybe I had not done a good enough job that day, so I would go through the day and redo it again in my mind. I would also overanalyze conversations to check if I had said the right things.

Time was such a huge factor for me, and I never felt like I had enough of it. I justified eating in the car as a way of saving time. I was usually late for things, because I do not like to waste time while waiting for someone or for an event to begin.

One of my hobbies is to read. However, I had to limit myself. When I started a book, I would continue to read it until it was finished, no matter how long it took. I would stay up for hours or entire nights just to finish a book.

I hated to shop because I had to go down *every* aisle, whether I needed something or not. If I did not do that, then I felt like I might have missed something that I needed. I knew this was ridiculous, because I even had to go down the pet food aisle. I did not need pet food—I did not own a pet!

I avoided malls because I felt I had to look in every store, even if I knew I was not going to need anything from a particular store. When I did buy something, such as an article of clothing, I would check ten other stores to be sure I got the best bargain. If not, then I would not be happy with my purchase and would obsess about it for months.

I wanted nothing more than to be married and have a family, but I was afraid. I was afraid of men and relationships. I knew so many unhappy married couples that it caused me to be afraid of marriage. I was afraid my husband might get sick and die. I was afraid my children would get terrible illnesses. I was afraid I would not know how to be intimate with my husband. I was afraid of being human…I was afraid of life.

I liked to keep myself very busy so I could not ruminate. I would fill my schedule and work until ten or eleven o'clock at night or until I reached exhaustion.

When I counted money, I had to recount it many times. When I wrote out checks, I proofread them over and over. I did not do anything halfway; it was either all or nothing. I thought in black or white—there was no gray.

My checking compulsions were taking two to three hours of my time every day, but they gave me comfort. After completing the rituals, a safe, warm feeling would come over me.

I used to sing in a church choir, but then I would get panic attacks that the floor would collapse and everyone would die. I was also afraid of intimacy—fearing a man would touch my body and feel my fat.

I did not trust anyone. So many people had disappointed me that I expected to be hurt or betrayed. If a job had to get done, then I liked to do it myself. If I was in a car, then I had to be the driver. I liked being in control, because I feared the unknown. I was afraid of things I had no control over. Food was the one thing I could control.

I was afraid of amusement park rides. The only rides I would go on were the bumper cars, because I could control them, but I always hated anyone bumping into me. I wanted to be in my own world.

I was afraid of flying, of putting my life into the pilot's hands. I had no trust. Even though I did not know how to fly, I would have felt safer if I had been the pilot.

I was socially backward. In a room full of strangers, I would stay by myself. If someone approached me, then I would talk, but I would not initiate a conversation. I would be especially nervous around males except for gay or married men. I would rather stay home than go out; I would rather be by myself than with people.

I could not keep food in my house. If I went food shopping, then I would put the groceries on top of the counter because I did not want the food messing up my cabinets.

Whatever I started had to be completed. I would go Christmas shopping December 24 and buy all my gifts in one day. The reason I waited so late was because I did not like the gifts messing up my home. When I ordered a pizza, I ate the whole thing. I did not like leftovers. If one of my nails broke, then I would bite off the remaining nine.

With the depression, I became inflexible and aloof. I experienced a loss of energy, interest, and concentration.

I was afraid of my mom dying. I was afraid I would die without having loved someone in my life.

I occasionally had sick, perverted thoughts. They really scared me until I read that this was normal for people with OCD.

I tried smoking in order to stop eating. I have asthma and am allergic to smoke, but I was willing to try anything. One day, I smoked an entire pack of cigarettes. Needless to say, I had an asthma attack.

In therapy, I learned that I needed to cut back on my compulsions. So I gradually cut back. I had to limit my rituals; for example, when crossing out items on my list, I would do it three times instead of eight. I still checked through my house, but I tried to do it only on weekends. I checked the curling iron and door lock once. I slept on my couch so I would not have to make my bed. On the way home, I stopped at one place to get food. I tried to stop working by 8:00 p.m., after which I would relax and watch television. I tried to be in bed by 10:30 p.m. I could not stop everything cold turkey—I could not even bear to think about that.

CHAPTER 9

THE ROAD TO RECOVERY

Once my depression was under control, I started working on curbing my OCD. I did a lot of researching, investigating, and reading. What I learned helped me to get on the path to healthy living.

OCD is an anxiety disorder in which a person is consumed by repetitive, unwanted thoughts (obsessions) or actions (compulsions) that he or she feels unable to stop or control. Most people with OCD have both obsessions and compulsions. They feel powerless to change their behaviors even though they know that the thoughts or behaviors are senseless. It is believed that an estimated 3 percent of the general population—as many as five million Americans—will experience symptoms of OCD at some point in their lives. I think this statistic is a little conservative, because I believe there are more people with OCD who are not aware of the disease or are ashamed of it. Therefore, it often goes unreported.

It is believed that OCD is caused by a chemical imbalance of serotonin, which acts as a messenger between nerve cells in the brain. Studies have also shown that there may be a genetic factor to OCD. That makes sense to me, because I strongly believe that my mother had OCD. This disease affects men and women equally, usually beginning in young adulthood. For me, it started around the age of thirteen.

Medicine helps to bring the symptoms of OCD under control, but it does not eliminate the underlying disorder. I will always have OCD, so I have to learn to manage it rather than to cure it.

An obsession is an intrusive thought. It is recurrent, unwanted, and inappropriate. There are different types of compulsions, which usually fall into one of the following categories: counting, checking, hoarding, repeating, cleaning, ordering, and ruminating. I discovered I suffered from all the types, some types more than others.

Approximately 75 percent of people with OCD will experience a major depressive episode at some point during their lives, and about one-third of people with OCD have symptoms of depression at the same time that they are having OCD symptoms. Common symptoms of depression include feelings of hopelessness, worrying, irritability, indecisiveness, and sleep problems.

For me, behavior therapy, along with medication, was the best course of action in treating my OCD. While in behavior therapy, I worked with my therapist to learn to understand, manage, and control my obsessions and compulsions. I had to find and face the things I feared; the official term for this is *exposure*. Then I had to refrain from carrying out the compulsive rituals, which is called *ritual or response prevention*. I was told it was best to experience the anxiety when it occurred rather than to fight it. Since most of my compulsions were mental images, I used the strategy of imagery practice. I visualized myself forgetting to do something and experienced the worst-case scenario. For example, I let myself imagine that I had left the front door unlocked. The worst thing that could happen was that I would be robbed, so I thought about all that went along with being robbed. Then I would tell myself I had insurance. I learned that if I waited it out, then my anxiety would diminish. I had to practice this every day. It was very difficult, but each day, the anxiety lessened.

I changed my thinking. I would tell myself that I had done my best, and that would have to be good enough. When I would write a check, I would tell myself that if it was wrong, then the bank would notify me.

I joined an OCD support group and found it to be very helpful. It was important for me to learn that there were other people suffering with the same type of problem.

My niece also helped me to heal. She loves me unconditionally. She has shown me I am capable of feeling and loving. She truly makes me happy.

CHAPTER 10

SUMMER OF 1998

The summer of 1998, I decided, was going to be my summer. I wanted to concentrate on getting healthy. With the depression and OCD under control, I knew it was time to face my toughest battle—my eating disorder.

I promised myself I would make a food shopping list, go shopping, and buy only nutritious food. I had made a deal with myself that I would not go to a fast-food restaurant for three months, and I had promised myself that I would eat only at home. I also began journal-writing again.

I became sad, as I knew I was losing my best friend. The only thing I had ever been able to depend on in my life, I was giving up. The only thing that had been with me to celebrate the good times as well as the bad had to stop. The drug I used to help numb my feelings had to be put down. The only thing I could completely control, I had to let go, and that was food. Food had become my companion, my lover. I felt a sense of loss.

I went to an amusement park at the beginning of the summer, but I could not fit on any of the rides. I tried one ride, and the man had to stop it, come over, and stretch the buckle. I was so embarrassed and humiliated that I did not go on any other rides.

I decided to go back to the gym, and I read a lot about healthy eating. I learned to eat smaller amounts and to eat five times a day. I learned to cut out caffeine, sugar, white bread, and alcohol. I tried not to worry about tomorrow or the future. I wanted to live for today.

As I kept thinking about my life, I made a list of reasons why I wanted to be thin:

- I wanted to be able to play with my niece without getting winded.
- I wanted to be healthier and lower my cholesterol.
- I wanted to be more attractive.
- I wanted to be able to do the physical things I used to do.
- I wanted to help my lower back.
- I wanted to be able to buy modern clothing.
- I wanted to have more confidence with my body.
- I wanted to live longer and feel better about myself.

As the summer progressed, I explored three avenues in search of a potential mate. Until this point, I had seen romance as something reserved for thin people—something I had to wait to enjoy until I was worthy of it. I turned my search into an experiment. With a dating agency and newspaper dating site, I noted I was heavy and received no phone calls. With the third newspaper ad, I did not mention my weight, and I received four phone calls in the first day.

Over the week, I called each of the men. The first man I called, I spoke to for forty-five minutes. We had a lot in common, and he told me he wanted to meet me. I then told him I was overweight. He said forget it and hung up the phone. I was not very upset, because I knew that this was his problem, not mine. I called the next man, and we talked for fifteen minutes. I decided then to tell him I was fat. He said he had a problem with it, so we hung up. Then I called the third person. We talked five different times before I finally told him I was overweight. He asked me how much I weighed, but of course, I did not tell him. He said he had to think about it. I should have told him no, but I did not.

We met a few days later at a bar and talked for over three hours. He walked me to my car and told me he could never get romantically involved with "a person of my size." He said he could easily fall in love with my personality but not my weight and that he was embarrassed to be seen with me. I went home, still not defeated. I felt good about myself, knowing I was a good catch. I am humorous, outgoing, well educated, honest, sincere, and financially secure. I considered it his loss, not mine.

So I continued and called the fourth person. After a few minutes, I decided to tell him I was full-figured. He said without hesitating that he did not have a problem with that.

I talked to over fifteen men from my personal ads. I expanded my search to include more than six different resources. I met so many people of all types and sizes. I did tell each of them I was overweight, and most did seem to mind, but I did not worry about it. My self-esteem rose immensely, and I felt like a teenager. I knew then that I was a "catch." Men were lucky to date me.

I used a lot of self-talk to keep myself on track. I knew I had to take little steps, and yet I wanted to lose 250 pounds by the end of the summer. I knew this was not realistic, but that was the all-or-nothing thinking. I thought five pounds was not good enough.

My eating habits improved. I was not so rigid in my thinking. I allowed myself fast food, cookies, and basically anything I wanted—occasionally. I did not obsess about food and ate only when I was hungry. People started to notice that I was losing weight.

Then, things started to spiral out of control. My family found out my mother had cancer, and I was devastated. I could not deal with the pressure, especially when she made a comment to me that she would not survive long enough to see me get married. I ate to block out the pain and guilt, feeling I had disappointed her.

Dad made me feel guilty about not spending enough time with my mom, even though I called her every day and went to see her once or twice a week. I hated going to the house, because my dad would always upset me, and we would end up arguing. He would tell me that I did not do enough for my mom and that I did not care. Then I would feel guilty and come home and binge with food.

I became the primary caregiver for my parents. As they started to depend more and more heavily on me, I felt there was no time for me. My stress level rose even higher, and I started to overextend myself again.

Then one day, rock bottom hit yet again. For the first time in a while, I thought about killing myself. Someone once said to be careful what you wish for because you just might get it. That happened to me.

I went from having no dates to having thirty dates over a three-week period. My goal was to find a boyfriend, and as with everything else I did, I gave it my all. After being stood up twice, my self-esteem started to fade. I saw many men I was supposed to meet drive by, take a look at me, and leave.

Then I met a man over the Internet. We talked on the phone for a week. He said he really wanted to meet me, but I was understandably hesitant. He was from another state and was willing to fly in for a weekend, but I was scared. I had to go to a conference and asked if he wanted to meet me there instead, so he agreed. I told him I was heavy; he told me he was also heavy.

We both made separate hotel reservations. This was different from any of my other dates. I was so nervous, but there was no turning back. I arrived at the hotel and met him in the lobby. He was very quiet, and I felt uncomfortable. I said I was going to check in, and he said he had to go to his car for his water. I checked in, turned around, and saw that he was nowhere to be found. I went to my room. After about a half hour, I finally accepted it. He had left. He drove for over two hours, saw me for half a second, and left. I felt so hideous-looking. I was crushed. I cried and wanted to kill myself. My heart was broken, my self-esteem shattered. I felt like I had been emotionally abused. I made a few phone calls and met a friend of mine who lived in the area.

I realized how tired and worn out I had made myself in my search. On some days, I would meet one guy for lunch, another for dinner, and still another for drinks. Between dates, I would take care of my parents and my house. Then I would go on the Internet until all hours of the night, driven to find myself a mate. I had switched compulsions.

As painful as this was, I did, however, learn many valuable lessons: you cannot make someone love you; you cannot let someone love you if you do not love yourself; your self-esteem is not determined by what others think about you; and you cannot hurry love.

CHAPTER 11

SUMMER OF 1999

Depression is mysterious. It disappears as quietly as it appears. I was not feeling well, and I had spent countless hours and a considerable amount of money going back and forth to doctors with no conclusions. I was out of breath, sweating, fatigued, and not sleeping; everyone thought it was because of my weight. I was given all different types of medications, but nothing worked. At times, I thought it was all in my head and just a part of my depression. It turned out that I had a sinus infection, which was causing a whole chain of events ending with asthma attacks. I had five attacks in one day. As a result, I ended up in the hospital.

During my stay, I became very depressed because I was alone. When my mom was in the hospital, my dad was by her side constantly. The same was true with my sister and brother-in-law. My friends came and visited, but that was not the same. I started to think about what would happen when I got older. Who would be there to take care of me?

A small part of me was to blame for these attacks. I was driven to find someone to love who would love me in return. I had switched compulsions and made myself exhausted.

I really wanted the men I dated to like me. I treated every date as if it were my last—just like I would treat each meal as if it were my last. I felt like I was trying to fill a cup with intimacy, but the cup had a hole in the bottom.

I got so depressed that my doctor suggested I see a specialist about getting my stomach stapled. I was scared and excited. I went to the appointment over Christmas vacation. I met the requirements for the surgery, so I signed up to have it done, but I left the office crying. The doctor had told me the most I could lose was one hundred pounds. That was not enough. The doctor also said I could never eat regularly again, and for about a year, I would have to eat teaspoonfuls of food. I loved eating, and I loved food! This was not what I wanted. Two weeks later, I canceled the surgery.

One positive thing I had going for me in my life was the fact that my weight was steady. I did not make the best choices, but I managed to eat only three meals a day with no snacks in between. I made a pro-and-con list about losing weight. The only con was that I would not be safe—someone could get close to me.

Another positive thing, ironically, was a result of my mom's illness. My mom and I became very close. For the first time, we uttered the words "I love you" to each other. We now say it every day. The rest of my family has even opened up, and we have at least some communication.

I decided to set a goal for myself. I wanted a tennis bracelet. It was impractical and frivolous—it was the perfect choice. I had always wanted a boyfriend or husband to buy me one, but I decided that since I had the means to buy myself one, I would. Every day I ate healthy, I would contribute five dollars to my bracelet fund. This helped me to stay focused. There were times when I would think about stopping at a fast-food place then told myself no. The pleasure from the food would last only a few minutes, but the bracelet would be mine forever.

As for my social life, during a session with my therapist, I said I did not know what scared me more—finding no one special in my life...or settling. I knew which men were not the ones for me and that I deserved more, but I used to think that since I was heavy, I would have to take whoever wanted me. I assumed I would not find an intelligent, funny, caring man because I did not deserve one.

Then one day, I just started to feel wonderful. The funny thing was that my life was not any different. My perspective just changed. I began cooking and eating at home. I was learning to keep my stress level down and managed to make time for myself. The man-hunt was over; I decided to let nature take its course. I was just going to enjoy being me—being happy.

Ruminating lists in my head had stopped. I was no longer checking every room in my house. I was putting food in my cabinets. I learned to leave my bed unmade and dishes in the sink. For me, these were huge accomplishments.

I started thinking in the present as opposed to the future. In the past, for example, I would be meeting a gentleman on a blind date, and I would have myself all worked up before I even met him. For example, I would think to myself that I knew this man had a dog. If we hit it off, then I was not sure about the dog. I am allergic to dogs, so if we got married, then the dog would have to go. Or maybe the dog could stay outside. Then I thought if he had to make a choice between the dog and me, then the dog would win. All of these crazy thoughts before I had even met the man!

The strangest thing for me was my new awareness of feelings: sadness, happiness, fear, anger, and the like. These feelings did not make me afraid, and I did not want to eat to stuff them. I *enjoyed* feeling. I felt alive!

I woke up one day and told myself I did not want to die. I knew I had been committing suicide using food, so I made an appointment with a doctor to get a prescription for a diet medication and to devise an exercise program to meet my needs. The doctor put me on a fat-absorbing pill that I had to take with each meal. I was very excited.

After two weeks, I fell and fractured a rib. I was told no exercise for six weeks. Then I was diagnosed with anemia, which added to my fatigue. In my life, the pattern had always been the same—take one step forward and end up two steps back.

Socially, I still spoke to men. Some of them would leave right after we met. I kept getting kicked when I was down, but I made myself get up. I knew I was a strong person. I had to be. And I was not settling.

I went back to church. While in confession, I told the priest I was angry with God. I was hurt because he had not sent me someone to love. The priest said that I had turned away from the one person who *did* love me unconditionally—God. I had never thought of it that way...

I wanted to work on my issues and escape my family's path of unhappiness. I wanted to make my own mistakes, not repeat theirs. I wanted to be happy and not pass down to my children or spouse unhealthy beliefs and/or practices.

I started going to the gym faithfully and eating healthy. I meditated fifteen minutes a day. Each day, I got stronger emotionally and physically. I learned that I deserved happiness. I focused on positive things. When I meditated, I thanked God for the small miracles that had happened to me during the day. My focus shifted. I was happy being who I was at that moment. I considered life as a journey, and I was hitting my share of potholes along the way.

I became proud of all I had overcome and accomplished. I knew I had a huge mountain to climb, but when I got scared, I just turned around and looked at how far I had come. My disease had made me a stronger person. They say God never gives you more than you can handle. Maybe he did not want to send someone special in my life until I realized how special *I* was first.

CHAPTER 12

SUMMER OF 2001

I love myself, and I am a great person. I know this now. For someone so intelligent, this was hard for me to understand, see, and accept.

I know I will always suffer from OCD, compulsive overeating, and at times, depression. This does not make me a weak person. A good thing is, now I can recognize immediately when my OCD is starting to act up. I get anxious, short-tempered, and tired. Then I start with the lists and working late nights. The difference is, since I recognize it, I can try to curb it. If I cannot do it on my own, then I call my therapist.

As of today, I have lost 130 pounds, and I am on my way to a healthy body to go along with my healthy mind. I was right. I had to let go of the weight obsession and work on my other issues first. That is what made this weight loss different from the ones before. I was not mentally ready before.

I have been dating a wonderful man for two years. He found me, and he accepts me for who I am. He is kind, smart, funny, and sweet. I am enjoying our relationship one day at a time. In the beginning, I had trouble believing his intentions. I thought he just wanted to make fun of me. Boy, was I wrong. He treats me like a queen and tells me that I am beautiful. And at last, I can accept his compliments.

I searched for happiness for thirty-four years, and here it was right in front of me the entire time. Happiness came from inside me. Things, people, and money could not make me happy. I had to be happy with me.

I have finally convinced myself that I am a great person regardless of my weight. When I started my journey, I entered an eating disorder clinic because I was so repulsed with my weight and what I looked like. I am five pounds heavier today than I was then, and I think I am beautiful. I just never saw it before.

All my life, I have been searching for love. The one place I failed to look was inside myself. I had always blamed others for not liking me because of my weight, but the truth was, I did not even like myself.

I have changed a lot over the years. I have learned to express my feelings. I have learned to accept myself. I have learned to feel my pain. I would love to tell you that I lived happily ever after, but that is not true. I still get lonely, depressed, and anxious. But with my strength, God's love, and friends to help, I take one day at a time. I now know that God did not make me different—just special. And whenever I feel down or think I cannot do it, I look at my beautiful tennis bracelet and smile.

CHAPTER 13

THE TWENTY-FIRST CENTURY—CAN THIS FINALLY BE THE TURNING POINT?

I t is amazing how life has its ups and downs. It is also sad how I always responded to both the happy and the sad times with food. Again, that stems back to my childhood. I do not want to blame everything on the past, because I am an adult and can make decisions on my own. But whenever my family was happy or sad, we ate to mark the event.

During February 2000, we found out my mom had a very rare form of cancer. It is so rare, in fact, that hers is the first case that was ever diagnosed while the patient was still alive. They used experimental drugs on her, and she went through hell. I took the brunt of caring for her and felt responsible for her. My sister had my niece to raise and a marriage to uphold, and my brother was very irresponsible. My dad told us over and over again how we never were doing enough for our mom. My weight rose higher and higher. After I went to see her—either after her multiple stays in the hospital or nursing homes—I would stop at the nearest fast-food place and/or convenience store and buy any type of junk food I wanted: cupcakes, ice cream, cheeseburgers, pizza, french fries, and so on. Then I would binge-eat until I was numb. I did this to suppress the feelings.

During this time, I met a nice gentleman who treated me great and looked past my weight. He loved me for who I was. My mom got to meet him, and she liked him. He got to "know" her but not the real her—just the shell of a sick woman in and out of nursing homes and hospitals. Finally, the phone call came that she had passed away. I was devastated. I had lost my mom.

Years later—even today—Dad says we never took care of her. He was the one who did not want to call the ambulance when she fell or got really sick at home, because he was worried about what the neighbors would think—always worried about what others would think. I am at peace that I did my part, however.

My boyfriend and I broke up shortly after that, and I started working toward my doctorate degree. This was a personal goal of mine, and I had always told my mom I would get my doctorate. Once again, my OCD and eating were out of control. I would still stop for food along the trip to college and on the way home. Doing assignments was hell, just as it had been when I was getting my graduate and undergraduate degrees, because I wanted to be perfect and would reread everything over and over again.

My boyfriend and I reconciled, and after a year, we got engaged. I was finally happy. It was then I decided to have gastric bypass surgery. I weighed my highest, which was around 380 pounds. I had the procedure done in New York and lost about one hundred pounds. I got married and thought I looked OK in my gown—but still very heavy. I wanted to lose more. (Remember, nothing was ever good enough.) I got a new job that I loved, and I completed my doctorate degree. I was very proud of myself.

My marriage was very rocky from the start. My husband changed almost immediately after I married him; he was not very good to me. I was not very happy, nor did I set any boundaries. I stuffed my emotions. We tried to get pregnant immediately, because I had always wanted a family and was not a young woman. After about a year and multiple tests, I discovered I could not have a child. I was devastated and stuffed my emotions even further.

We decided to go the route of adoption. Without the money for an international adoption, we went through a service agency. It was a horrible experience, and we nearly had to give our son back multiple times because the biological parent would not terminate his rights. When he finally did, he tried to revoke them. I stuffed my emotions, and my weight went even higher. The adoption finally went through, and we had a beautiful son. Needless to say, I gained all my weight back. The weight loss surgery did not work.

CHAPTER 14

SUMMARIZING MY LIFE STRUGGLES

They say God does not give you more than you can handle. I often wonder why he had to give me so much. But each and every thing he gave me has made me the strong person I am today. I wanted to write this book to give at least one person hope that you can do it. I finally found peace at the age of forty-seven. It took that long. I am hoping that by reading my book, it will not take you as long.

Growing up, as you have read, was not easy for me. As punishment for me when I was "bad," my dad would hit me with a strap. I know I was not a bad kid and did not deserve it. Due to my experience, I have never touched my son as a form of punishment.

I had medical problems as a child. One was that I had severe hip pain in the eighth grade. The doctors would not do anything about it; they just said to lose weight. If they had treated this, then perhaps I would not have the problems I have today with my back. I also had allergies and asthma, to name a few other medical issues.

I was bullied all the time—not just in school but out in public as well. It was so difficult and hurt so badly.

Going to college and never fitting in was not fun. I had been raised to think that seeking out help was a sign of weakness and that it was not for someone educated, which made me feel even worse.

Living on my own and wanting a boyfriend/family more than ever was horrible. Feeling lonely is terrible. I had to learn to be happy with myself first. I had to learn someone else could not make me happy.

Marrying the first person who showed a real interest in me was not the answer. Even though he treated me really well in the beginning, after we got married, he became verbally abusive. I took it because I believed I did not deserve better or could not find someone else. I considered divorce about one hundred times but did not have the courage to go through with it. On the 101st, though, I finally did it and filed.

Discovering I could not have a child naturally was devastating. That was a hard pill to swallow. Going through the adoption process was a living hell. Although it took two years and turned out to be the best thing that ever happened to me, it was a horrible road to travel.

My jobs along the way had some bumps. One coworker tried to bully me into doing something unethical. He was the president of the union, so I went above his head because I stuck to my ethics. I worked in a political environment but was not political. I was always ethical and held to my values.

I continued to have medical problems. Besides three back surgeries, I also had other surgeries. I currently take about thirty medications for about twelve different medical conditions. I have learned to accept it.

I can go and on with all I have to deal with in my life. I have persevered. I am proud of that. I got help. I should have stuck with therapy in my twenties, but I guess I was not ready. Do not live your life with "should have" or "could have," or you will drive yourself crazy. You can overcome adversity. Just look forward. The next chapter explains how I finally made it.

CHAPTER 15

WHAT MADE ME FINALLY MAKE IT

I *Am Out of the Closet, and I Am Not Even Gay*—that was the original title of this book. I am not afraid now to tell people that I see a psychologist and that I have OCD. I no longer have to deal with the stigma that my parents instilled in me and that I once believed. I will always have OCD, even when it is controlled. I will always suffer from depression from time to time, and I need to recognize it and keep it under control. I will always be an anxious person. This is the hand I have been dealt. This is the cross I have to bear, and I am at peace with it. There are many others out there like me; I am not a freak. I am very successful, but I will always have to see a psychologist and therapist.

I cannot tell you my life is wonderful. My dad, at eighty-two, is still very critical of my siblings and me. That will never change. The difference is my response to him. I do not respond with bad food choices, and I have boundaries. I am kind of like Superman. Dad's comments deflect off me—they do not penetrate.

My marriage is not wonderful. To say it is difficult at times is being kind. My husband can be a hothead and treat me rotten and then two minutes later be nice as pie. I used to respond by eating the wrong foods. I filed divorce papers to let him know I was not taking his nonsense. I now have boundaries and do not put up with it. In the past, I would respond with food, but now I do not.

Being a parent is difficult. I want to be perfect. (It is that all-or-nothing thinking again.) Sometimes I get so frustrated with my son, and then I feel guilty for it. But he also brings me much joy.

I have my own medical issues as well. I had back surgery three times, resulting from multiple car accidents—and probably from being overweight most of my life and not taken seriously by doctors. I also have a whole gamut of other medical issues. One thing I am most proud of, though, is that I never give up.

I have a wonderful therapist, Maryann. I have been seeing her for ten years, and I suspect I will be seeing her for the rest of my life. She has helped me tremendously. I also see a great psychologist, Brad, who has listened to me and prescribed the right combination of medications without judging. I take medicines for depression, anxiety, and OCD, as well as ones to help me sleep and for other ailments, and I had to go through many psychologists to find the right one. The right support group is also a key element.

I currently leave my house unkempt, my bed unmade, and my mats in my car dirty. I do not clean my plate when I eat and recognize when I am full. These are huge accomplishments. What worked for me? I did what was the hardest thing for me in my life—I cut out carbohydrates and sugars. I realized I was addicted to them both, and they had caused my obsessive overeating. Being Italian, I was raised on pizza, pasta, and bread, so this, for me, was extremely difficult. But I wanted to live. I was 387 pounds when I gave up carbs and sugars. I had lost one hundred pounds eating healthy prior to giving them up, but the weight was starting to creep back.

My problem was that I was obsessive about everything. One time, I ate so many carrots that my feces were orange! I would binge on healthy *or* unhealthy food. Even on the low-carb diet, you could have peanuts, almonds, and pork rinds. Even though you do not count calories on this weight-loss program, I had to cut these items out because I would eat the entire contents of the package. However, I would not binge on protein or allowable vegetables.

I am down now to 158 pounds and have lost a ton of inches thus far. I do not crave sweets or carbohydrates, and I know I can never go back to eating either one again. My sugar levels are very good (I was on my way to becoming a diabetic), and my cholesterol is very good as well.

I am not saying this way of eating will work for you. What I *am* saying is that I am a compulsive overeater, and the carbohydrates and sugars triggered me to eat more. Hunger had nothing to do with eating for me, and since eliminating those items from my diet, the compulsions have stopped. The weight also came off quickly. I found support on social media. And I have accomplished this with no exercising, which I do not recommend, but because of my back, it was necessary for me. I have never been healthier, and my depression and anxiety are under control most of the time.

My advice to you is that you can overcome anything. No matter how bad things are, they will get better. Get help; get someone to talk to. If you need medication, then do not stop until you find what works for you. Taking care of yourself should be your number one priority, because you are worth it. Stay away from negative people. Be positive. Love yourself.

CHAPTER 16

POEMS FROM THE HEART

The following are poems I wrote in my twenties and thirties as I struggled. You will recognize the themes.

A Fool in Love

Nobody knows,
nobody understands,
this pain I feel when you are around.
Your memory still lingers deep in my heart.
This hurt won't go away.
It doesn't want to stop.

You push me aside like I'm not even alive.
But why do I always come back
loving you more than ever before?
I guess I'm just a fool in love.

I put on this act and pretend not to care.
But it's time to face the fact.
Your memory will always be there.

Others are seen in the eyes of you,
which only adds to this pain and
leaves me feeling blue.

Enough tears have been shed
and nights spent dreaming of you.
It's time it all came to a halt.
I have to face it.
We will always be apart.

I know that time
will heal the wounds,
and the memories will eventually fade.
But there will always be a
piece of you
deep in my heart,
a piece that
will always remain.

Love

Sometimes I get so confused
feeling like I'm being used.
I put on my mask
and continue to act
all happy and amused.

I've had my share of ups and downs.
I guess I shouldn't complain.
But sometimes everything
piles up, which includes this pain.

I have shared my laughter and my tears
with my friends throughout the years.
And thank God for my friends for
without them, I couldn't be
half the person that I am.

But there are times when I need
something more,
a lover, a friend,
a man and a boy.
Someone to take care of
and someone to hold.
Someone to share myself with
and someone to grow old.

A good love is like true gold,
valuable and sparkling.
But if it is fake,
it is worthless
and dull.
But I guess that's the risk
one has to take.

Untouched

I see you
and my stomach quivers.
I see you
and my heart pounds.
I see you
and my eyes swell with tears.

Why do I feel this way?
Can this be love?

I question it because
you see me
and you ignore.
You see me
and you run away.
You see me
and pretend not to care.

Why do you feel this way?
Can this be hate?

If you were to
see me for who I am
then this could be love.
But what we have
is a woman in love
and
a man untouched.

Who I Am

My shape is not perfect
and my body is plump.
Why don't men look twice at me
or attempt to get to know
the person behind the fat,
the part that makes me?

It hurts to see
others love and not me.
I hide behind my wall
always smiling and laughing
while inside I am frowning and sad.

Is it the embarrassment,
the shame, or the pride that
makes you laugh at me
while inside I cry?

Many tears I have shed
over jokes and boys alike
but not anymore
because now my heart is closed to love.
No man can come near me now
the wall I've built is strong.

Maybe someday I'll lose the weight
and regain my self-esteem.
And when I meet a man,
I hope he will love me
not for being fat or skinny
but for being me.
After all, that's the person
who I am.

Risks

How do you tell someone you love how you really feel,
those feelings that go beyond friendship,
that extend deep in the heart and are real?

How do you tell someone you love how you really feel,
without risking the loss of the friendship
because he doesn't feel the same as you feel?

How do you tell someone you love how you really feel,
without risking being hurt and ridiculed,
feeling ashamed and brokenhearted?

I guess one has to ask, is it better to gain
both a friend and a lover with the risk
of losing the friend or to just keep the
friendship and risk nothing?

But then one has to ask without risks,
can there be love?

So how do you tell someone you love how you really feel?
You just risk it, tell them,
and be real.

Snow

Snow is a funny thing.
People want it to snow
and are disappointed
when it does not.

But if there is too much snow
it becomes ugly,
hated, and the excitement
is gone.

But if there's just the right amount of it,
snow becomes beautiful,
breathtaking,
soft,
appreciated.

Is this snow that I speak of,
or is this love?

Snowfall

Like a snowfall,
my love for you
is some days too much
some days not enough
and some days not at all.
It never is just right.

Like a snowfall,
my love for you
is free to come,
but it's unrequited
which isn't right.

Like a snowfall,
my love for you
will eventually stop,
melt, and be no more.

Unrequited Love

I found out today
how you really feel.
The reasons you've
been hiding from and
not confiding in me.

Tears swelled in my eyes
my heart tore apart
when I opened the door
and saw her there,
the former girl,
your past love,
my future pain.
It broke my heart
knowing it was over
before it even began.

You said you two were through.
There was nothing between
you and her.
I believed you.
Oh, what a fool I've been.

It was my fault,
for making something
out of nothing.
For thinking things could be
just as my mind had planned.

Well, now I know.
I found out the hard way.
And my heart will pay dearly
the price of unrequited love.

Nothing

Risks are what make life interesting.
Risks are what make life painful.

To reach out to love
is to risk rejection.
To convey one's feelings
is to risk ridicule.
To want more
is to risk friendship.
To keep dreaming
is to risk a broken heart.

But without risks,
there could be no love.

To risk nothing is
to have nothing,
be nothing,
love nothing.

Friends We Should Be

Why don't you call
after all we've been through?
Aren't you happy with me
as I am with you?

I know we're just friends
and that's OK.
But I thought something
might grow,
something better you know.

Dreams and memories
of what you said and did,
those times we've shared
keep me going.

But sometimes my mind wonders,
anticipating,
will he phone? Is he home?
Who's he with?
Is it over?
I want to shout,
"Don't shut me out!"

Those love songs on the radio
leave me feeling blue,
and every minute is spent
thinking of you.

I love you, you know.
Just look deep in my eyes.
I can't hide it and I won't
deny it, will you?

I know there's something
you feel for me.
Is it pity? Dear God,
I hope not.

We were good together,
you and me.
At least friends we should be.
Who knows?
I guess I'll have to wait and see.

I Believe

Dear God,
what have you got planned for me?
I know when I am feeling down,
when I think I cannot sink any lower,
you always manage to show me a sign,
to lift my spirits and
help me to hold on.

Some days I feel so lonely.
I want someone to love me
and someone I can love.
I want a husband and a family.
I know this sounds selfish,
me wanting so much.

But I also know I have to be patient,
because eyes have not seen,
ears have not heard
what God has ready
for those who love him.

I love you, God, and I believe.

Love

Empty promises.
Little white lies.
Words without meaning.
Talk just to talk.
Listen without hearing.
Love just to love.
Lack of feeling.
Lack of caring.
Hurtful responses.
Say what you mean.
Mean what you say.
Express what you feel.
Love along the way.

ABOUT THE AUTHOR

Dr. Marianne C. Joyason has struggled with compulsive overeating, obsessive-compulsive disorder (OCD), depression, and anxiety for most of her life. She continually works toward better mental health and has overcome many challenges.

Joyason lives with her son in the northeastern United States.